the Goddess monologues

Vandana Khanna

ISBN: 978-1-939728-08-1
Diode Editions
Doha, Qatar

Cover art, design & layout: Law Alsobrook

Ordering & Contact information:
http://www.diodeeditions.com

Acknowledgments: .

Grateful acknowledgment is made to the editors of the following publications
in which these poems originally appeared, sometimes in earlier forms:

> *32 Poems* "A world like this hates a girl," & "Novice"
> *Connotation Press: An Online Artifact* "Parvati Practices Her Austerities"
>   & "Parvati Laments Her Reincarnation"
> *Crab Orchard Review* "We Are Always the Girls," "Parvati Rewrites Myth,"
>   "Sita in Exile," & "Goddess Re-Made"
> *Diode* "Krishna's Mother Advises," & "Sati"
> *The Journal* "In Captivity, Sita Contemplates Fidelity"
> *Linebreak* "Goddess Left Behind"
> *Memorious* "Why Sita Is Chosen," & "Parvati Fails the First Test of Being Holy"
> *The Missouri Review* "The Goddess Reveals What It Takes To Be Holy"
> *New England Review* "Monologue for a Goddess in Her First Incarnation,"
>   & "Goddess in the Dark"
> *Prairie Schooner* "Sita's First Kiss with Suburban Landscape," "Destruction Myth,"
>   & "Because you forgot me, I am weird in the world"
> *Passages North* "Prayer to Recognize the Body"
> *Redivider* "Goddess Out of Favor"

Prayer to Recognize the Body

There must be a word for this
heart-growing, to explain these teeth,

stinging skin like a gift, tremble of
hair coaxed from sweat and scalp.

The next thing I covet. the third eye's
velvet blink, the green pulse in my veins

of a forest I can't make myself step out of.
And what of all the things remade, swabbed

free of salt? Because who can tell
the difference in the dark between

antlers and branches and bone, between
the thick-haired chest of an animal and you.

Monologue for a Goddess in Her First Incarnation

Invent me in the half-opened eye
of night, stripped down to the brown
of my mind, the wind at my back,

a dark claw. Tell me again
I am unforgettable: face losing
its composition— skin the blue

of a stranger, spine whittled
to shadow, to hum, until I am
a see-through goddess. Undone,

my body can't remember itself:
somber knots and stem, bright stalks
of bone. Husband, for you, I go to pieces.

We Are Always the Girls

Our goodness measured, laid out
at night for the animals to practice on.
Our hurts hung from the trees.

We are always the girls, hushed,
hated—daughters born of some
monster. Nothing to recommend us,

with instructions hennaed on our backs,
a trail of wants that curves and hooks
around the long finger of our spines.

They chant for us to go away, to die
with their prim lips pursed, the shudder
of our stories on their tongues.

Our blood runs the green of tangled
vines, heartbeat of a thousand blackbirds.
Our veins opened by flame.

We turn away from their eyes to do
our sin, lick the salt from our palms.

Why Sita Is Chosen

Amongst peacocks and jacaranda
she is humble, calls everything leaf, bird, sky.

The forest left its branches in her chest,
mobbed her dreams with its noise, its fisted heat.

She is always in the wrong season, wakes
to a mouth full of pine needles, winter grass,

imagines the cold hush of stars, spiked and luminescent,
as halo, as proof. She is wary of fire, backing away

from stove, candle, match. In mirrors, she sees only
a mouth yielding, practices bending to the wind.

Sita's First Kiss with Suburban Landscape

In our seventh incarnation, we find
each other, yellowed shoulders in sunlight,
husked throats swollen with new breath.
Our mouths meet in small disasters.

Tethered by fence and sidewalk, we wait
for a lotus to bloom from your navel, glossy-
leafed and puckered in the sweating air.
You taste of all the people you've already

been, salted stubble, clean field of forehead.
Blank-palmed and desperate, our pollen-
dusted faces against suburban sky, skin
lit by swallowed stars. Abandoned

to an unruly yard, we are destined to repeat—
lips then sky, then fume of mosquitoes
in the prickled heat of the porch until, we
become a restless haze of honeysuckle and wasp.

Parvati Practices Her Austerities

The first thing to go: the word soft,
the clean teeth of a comb, the color red.

Then, I forget what I look like, or don't care:
weave twigs in my hair for clips, make believe

mushrooms are pearls, sheathe my feet
in slippers of dried mud. I teach myself

to hold the hum of OM in my lungs until
I'm holy, until you open your eyes and notice.

So you can see I am an empty bowl careful
with my wanting. I can wind the hot gnaw

of hunger into a tight spool, a body ready
to snap, ready to sing any song you want

from the thin reed of my throat. My narrowing
shoulders proof of all I've given up. Look for me:

a girl in a white sari the color of bone, a girl wrung
free of this world. Tell me this time I'll get what I want.

Krishna's Mother Advises

Watch out for the one with pink cheeks,
with wrists that can twist to music.
She wants you for the wrong reason:
the way the blue of your skin reminds
her of the sky after a monsoon.
No matter how much rain,
the color stays the same.

The cows rustle in the bleached hills,
in soft tufts of grain, urging you to resist
her tender shoulder, the smooth slope of back.
Resist her slim ankles, her milk-scent, her wonder.

You can name every flower, every animal
in the darkening forest, and she, simple,
only calls out the obvious—marigold, peacock, bull.

In Captivity, Sita Contemplates Fidelity

I search the bleak sky for shine.
The thin prickle of my thoughts
pecked by days of jungle rain—
the sound of waiting a white blur.

What is the color of devotion?
Purple night. Greened jungles,
yellow marigold dust.

I will not let anyone touch me.
My knotted hair imagines itself
a slick river in your hands, the pleats
of my sari, crisp and patient.

I refused that monkey you sent
to find me. My rescue is yours:
through meadow and forest,
wide-armed branches snatching
at your back.

Once, you pulled the stars
closer so we could feel
their humid skin after monsoon—
our fingers wet, melancholy.

Husband, every night is yours:
fill it with the tight snap of bow,
the hollow whistle of arrows on fire.

When I close my eyes, I can hear
the black burning from the sky.

The Goddess Left Behind

How easy to be left for damsel: to lie in a forest
for days, unseen, on a bed of thick needles
and not get pricked. Hold time in place under her
tongue, hold the last flower of air in her chest
to see what will happen—what will bloom and wilt.

When a girl can dream and not be frightened
of the years ahead of her yet to be lived, alone
in myrtle and moss. When she can see the animal's
teeth for its shine and not for the bite, the hurt
it leaves on her.

The crows mournful at the mouth of the cave
she reads as a sign of leaving: the world empty
of her. She of clipped wings, glistening with drama,
so pretty to look at, so stiff with misuse.

Parvati Laments Her Reincarnation

My body a revision of bones and skin,
face a dim-lit moon looking for its place
in the sky. How many times must we

rewind, start the story over? The stink
and heat of a wife's work stuck to my skin,
then you—smelling distant, of moss

and meadow. Each time we meet
something gets subtracted: the peculiar
beat of my blood, the browned husks

of my eyes. Read my palm, tell me where
to stand. Lie and say you hear the river
rushing through me, vein by vein.

Novice

No one wished me well: too plain
or too pretty, sadness buzzing around
me like a hot swathe of wasps.

I was the wrong wife, the wrong goddess,
last in line, a trophy pinned with dead
flowers and scorn—examined by moonlight,

flashlight, the gaps between my bones
gathering to a weak glimmer. Try, but no
chant could keep me in my place, nothing

as easy as us tied together, my clothes
to yours—the gold on my wrists the color
of lion, tight as teeth. My body dimwit,

dim-lit, the smell of a struck match, a charring:
one flash, one flame. Then: a light, alight.
I can't pray for what I don't know.

Parvati Fails the First Test of Being Holy

A shivering under my skin
made me doubt, made me want
to lie down in the grass with you.

I was a page folded over, late blooming
and slim-shouldered, always getting
it wrong: couldn't remember

which hand held the sickle, which
the trident, left my blessings to rust
in the rain. Ruined by nothing

but my thoughts, I wanted to be plain
and unconditional so I could slip
unnoticed between this world

and the next—so I could dream
a body of my own: clever bones,
a new flutter for the heart.

Instead, I wilt every prayer you put
in my mouth. Petal-soft, it crumples
easily in my tongue's mean curl.

Sati

*Hindu Goddess for whom the practice of a widow throwing
herself on her husband's funeral pyre is named*

My heart is no lantern.
No matter what they tell you,
it's not all marigolds and Ram, Ram
like some Hindu cheerleading chant.

At first, all I wanted was fire:
soot-lined skin, my hair in needles
of light and heat, the tight fist
of lungs like a blazing hive.

Red flame, blue flame—it was all the same.

But then, right before my bones
flared like torchlight, singed fingertips
smoothed to a shine, I thought
of the cool cusp of the moon,

river water soothing my throat,
contracting around me—
a muddy womb. Muck and silt
lining my mouth like a new word

for smoke, for freedom.

Instead I have cinder, all this
useless ash cupped into
the curve of my body, sitting
on my skin for an eternity.

Destruction Myth

A bride's ransom of tangled sari, skin
that holds the hush of loam and leaf,
the soil's damp-breathed kiss. Once,

I was untouched and still you asked for proof:
my feet on fire-threaded coals—soft
as lotus petals. Pressed into the ground

until I dissolve into hair, silt, cloth.
A lucky girl: blessed by gravel and dust,
a pretty neck strung with pebbles.

My virtue: a heavy hem pulled down,
dirty blooms choked into the slender vase
of my throat. Bury me with my hurt:

skinned and spare, with my voice:
the soot of black strands, flecked bone.

Goddess in the Dark

You kept me hidden in a drawer of wilt
and weeds, seeds sprouting sour: where
you left the tiger, the ash, our story.

Fire always the prerequisite to love.

What a way to treat a lady. I stayed midnight
to midnight, the air a stubborn gem of black.

Bowed my head, practiced how to hold
the shattered bowl of the moon in my hands.

The silver sprigs of light slipping through
the weave of my fingers I mistake for holiness.

I never catch enough to make it day.

The thorn's deft nips in the dark mark
our love in hot scratches, leave my

happiness scabbed, tough to the touch.
I choke down my prayers, the only
way I know how to be.

Because you forgot me, I am weird in the world

Already I've changed—wallflower, paper flower,
hidden and pressed. My mouth a thin-slotted
door, an opening in the brush. Find the spot
on my neck where the evil eye can leer

unhindered. The forest crowds around me
to stare, blank-eyed, free of conscience,
those eyes see what I've become: a bride's
narrow fingers, my hair a bereft knot

looking for solace. I know how to tidy
my heart, bite my tart tongue until it silvers
in my mouth. The crows' black song circles
overhead, calling me out, calling me lost.

Goddess Out of Favor

The animals love you less and less.
They can eye a girl as she is meant

to be—burning like her own planet.
You ate leaves until your jaw ached

with ash, your spinster shoulders set
against the wind. You buried the names

you were once called beneath the brush.
It was never enough to fill the hole

your doubt dug. All those false steps
around the fire meant nothing. No one

held you up to the light, no sadness
glistened on your lips the pretty

color of persimmons. No one cared
when you walked into the forest

raw and rustling like sugar cane,
your pulse thick with bees.

A world like this hates a girl

on her own, spider-webbed, bones
all out of place, a rented heart
on the fritz. There was one browner
than me, pushed into the corner
of the forest, ginger and bitter roots
growing at her ankles.

You white-washed, all halos and bees
and time, me with my pried-open prayers,
mouth full of ash—all I wanted:
a bit of red on my lips, someone
to smooth the sharp thorn of my hair,
a body that hums in contrary light.

I can pull the stars, their bright aching
from the sky but I can't dream all
the leaves back onto the trees.

Sita in Exile

Before the forest, giving in was easy:
my hands for your prayers, my skin
for your mouth. But once your doubt
grew taut, it was all fire: my ruin begun

in dirt and rubble, fourteen years
of leering branches, of stars plotting
against me. Now, I sleep alone in the sweat
of the afternoon, waken to an evening

of peeled purple. I bless all that is seen
and unseen with river water and bucket:
under the rough rope of my hair,
in the quiet between arms and thighs.

Gaunt as a paper fan, I wander the walled
garden in naked feet, pull my melancholy
close, a numb shawl. I beckon the tiger
to come and lick my ankles free of ash.

Parvati Rewrites Myth

I won't miss the dirty hive of your hair,
your slow drone of a chant that lasts all day.
In this version, I'm done with kindness,

left it in my last life, with my cheap glass bangles
and cotton sari. I am my own constellation
of pathetic stars, built my loneliness twig by twig—

lit it on fire to keep me warm. I can't pretend
to care even as the butter burns to clear, even as
I never learned the names of trees. Spiteful in white,

I've lost the bride's red parting my hair, the gold
at my ankles. Enough with all this jungle, with its
shiny tongues, sloppy mouth. I'll leave you

to your cave, your brilliance, spit your name out
like paan from my cheek—walk out of the tight cluster
of trees, the sun's hot tone on my head like a drum.

The Goddess Re-Made

You found me with night in my teeth—
a cheap date in need of a heart, a story,
a glass bangle in green. Any small mercy.

And I took it, leaving behind those
moaning cows, the thatched roofs
one lightening storm away from igniting.

You took inventory—breath and pulse,
cells and teeth, a numb womb.

You couldn't shake the river out of me,
so there it stayed, muddying my blood,
blurring the blink of my eyes.

Build me better—a girl with a spine
stiff as bark, a mouth refusing to part,
the brittle twig of ribcage.

Build me until there is nothing
soft left, nothing pink.

The Goddess Reveals What It Takes To Be Holy

Every girl wants to be post-sadness,
post-jungle so don't be fooled
by the cloak the color of heaven,
by petals perpetually at your feet.

To be the favorite, you have to
give in: clip on a smile, sweep
the floor with your hair, let him
call you by the wrong name.

Repeat after me: I'll hurt for you,
I'll domestic for you.
This requires constancy:
to shun, to burn, to look ugly

in white. Keep quiet, even as
the world is ending—hearts
skipping beats, histories peeled
off of your palms, line by line:

first love, then life. Full of doubt,
you must be content with stitching
your own wounds, buffing your scars
to a blinding gleam.

credit: Julia Dillon

Vandana Khanna was born in New Delhi, India and attended the University of Virginia and Indiana University, where she earned her MFA. Her first collection, *Train to Agra*, won the Crab Orchard Review First Book Prize and her second collection, *Afternoon Masala*, was the co-winner of the 2014 Miller Williams Arkansas Poetry Prize. Her work has appeared in the *New England Review, The Missouri Review, 32 Poems* and *Prairie Schooner* as well as the anthologies *Raising Lilly Ledbetter: Women Poets Occupy the Workspace, Asian American Poetry: The Next Generation* and *Indivisible: An Anthology of Contemporary South Asian American Poetry*.